A LITTLE GIANT® B

TONGUE TWISTERS

Mike Artell & Joseph Rosenbloom

Drawings by Mike Artell & Dennis Kendrick

STERLING

New York / London
www.sterlingpublishing.com/kids

Library of Congress Cataloging-in-Publication Data Available

LOT#: 10 9 8 7 6
08/12

Published by Sterling Publishing Co., Inc.
387 Park Avenue South, New York, NY 10016
Portions of the book excerpted from *World's Toughest Tongue Twisters* © 1986 by
Joseph Rosenbloom;
New material © 1999 by Mike Artell.
© 2005 by Sterling Publishing Co., Inc.
Distributed in Canada by Sterling Publishing
c/o Canadian Manda Group, 165 Dufferin Street
Toronto, Ontario, Canada M6K 3H6
Distributed in the United Kingdom by GMC Distribution Services,
Castle Place, 166 High Street, Lewes, East Sussex, England BN7 1XU
Distributed in Australia by Capricorn Link (Australia) Pty. Ltd.
P.O. Box 704, Windsor, NSW 2756, Australia

Sterling ISBN-13: 978-1-4027-4974-2
        ISBN-10: 1-4027-4974-0

For information about custom editions, special sales, premium and
corporate purchases, please contact Sterling Special Sales
Department at 800-805-5489 or specialsales@sterlingpub.com.

Before You Begin

How do you say a tongue twister correctly? There are two rules. First, tongue twisters must be said fast. You can say any tongue twister without stumbling if you say it slow enough. The trick is to say it fast—the faster the better.

The second rule is that most tongue twisters need to be repeated a certain number of times. If the tongue twister is several sentences long—let's say, the size of a paragraph—you only need to say it once in order to succeed (but remember to say the words fast!).

If the tongue twister is less than a sentence long, say it at least three times. (Those short tongue twisters are usually listed three times in the book.)

The tongue twisters in these pages have been chosen because they are hard to say. In fact, they include all the toughest tongue twisters in the world—or anyway the toughest ones we could find. (We also slipped in a few that weren't so tough, but that were so funny or so great or so silly that we couldn't resist them.)

Why pick such tough tongue twisters? Because the rougher they are, the funnier they are. Turn to any page in this book and you'll find your tongue doing ridiculous things. It will slip, slide, hesitate, get thick, get thin, and finally tangle up completely, and that's fun. It makes you laugh.

Try them out, Better yet, ask your friends to try them. Why not share the fun?

Ape cakes, grape cakes.
Ape cakes, grape cakes.
Ape cakes, grape cakes.

Andrea and Andrew ate eight acid apples accidentally.

Angus' angry answer annoyed
Angie's aunt. Angus is always
annoying Angie's aunt.
Angus actually enjoys annoying
Angie's aunt. It's awful, although
Angie's aunt only acts annoyed.

If I assist a sister-assistant, will the sister's sister-assistant assist me?

"What ails Alex?" asks Alice.

The little addled adder added ads.

9

Abbie's Aunt Annie isn't answering Abbie's Aunt Amy.

TIME CHALLENGE

*How many times can you
say this in 10 seconds?*

Ada made a 'gator hate her,
so the 'gator ate her.

YUM!

All artists aren't artful.
There are artful artists
and awful artists.
Although there are a lot
of awesome artful artists,
annoying awful artists
occur more often.

Angels hang ancient anchors at angles that anger ogres.

Arnie's oranges aren't as orange as Arnold's oranges.

Are there auks in the Arctic
or aren't there auks in the Arctic?
And if there are auks in the
Arctic, are they auctioning arks?

Ava ate eighty eggs.
Ava ate eighty eggs.
Ava ate eighty eggs.

Abe and Babe will grab a grub
from Greg. Will Abe and Babe
grab a grub from Greg? If Abe
and Babe will grab a grub from
Greg, where's the grub from
Greg Abe and Babe will grab?

All Al's sly allies lie.

Al's ally is in the alley.

Adele is a dull adult.

Aunt Edith's anteater ate Aunt Edith's ants.

Eight apes ate Nate's tape.

Never ever offer awful Arthur alfalfa.

Ann Anteater ate Andy
Alligator's apples,
so angry Andy Alligator ate
Ann Anteater's ants.

Adam ate an autumn apple.

Alice asks for axes.
Alice asks for axes.
Alice asks for axes.

Ancient anchors anchor ancient arks.

Can an active actor always
actually act accurately?

Are Archie and Audrey's
archery arrows as arty as
Artie's archery arrows?

Ashley's leaping as she's sleeping.

A man demanded Amanda's panda.

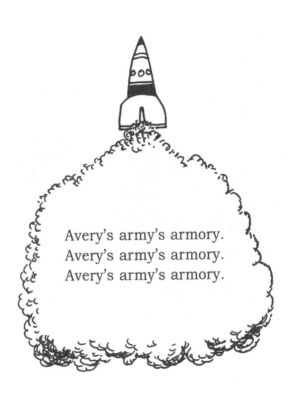

Avery's army's armory.
Avery's army's armory.
Avery's army's armory.

Big boxes of bears being brought aboard.

Rubber baby-buggy bumpers.
Rubber baby-buggy bumpers.
Rubber baby-buggy bumpers.

Once upon a barren moor
There dwelt a bear; also a boar.
The bear could not bear the boar,
The bear thought the bear a bore.
At last the bear could bear no more
That boar that bored him on the moor.
And so one morn he bored the boar—
that boar will bore no more!

HEE
HEE

Beware! That's a bear lair.
I wouldn't go in there on a dare.
In there is where a bear scared Pierre.
Pierre was not aware of the bear in the
lair until the bear gave a glare and Pierre
ran from there.

A big bug hit a bold bald bear and the
bold bald bear bled blood badly.

The Bold Bald Bear

Who bit the bold bald bear on the shoulder on the boulder and made the bold bald bear on the boulder bawl?

Brandy bandaged the bear.

Bobby Bear's B-B bean shooter.
Bobby Bear's B-B bean shooter.
Bobby Bear's B-B bean shooter.

The big bloke bled in the big blue bed.

Brenda Black was blameless.

Betty better butter Buddy's
brother's bagel. But before
Betty butters the bagel, Betty
better boil and bake the bagel.

Bruce brought big biscuits.
Bob brought both briskets.

A box of biscuits,
a box of mixed biscuits,
and a biscuit mixer.

Blake the baker bakes black bread.

The bottom of the butter bucket
is the buttered bucket bottom.

"The bun is better buttered,"
Buffy muttered.

Bring the brown baked bread back.

Brian's bride bakes buns, but
Brian buys baked bread.

Aiken Bacon was baking bacon.
The bacon he was bakin' was
bought in Macon. So he was
makin' baked Macon bacon.

Bill blows big blimpy bubbles.
When Bill's big, blimpy
bubbles burst,
Bill began to blubber.
Bill was a big blimpy baby.

Betty Block blows big black bubbles.

A bachelor botched a batch
of badly baked biscuits.
Did the bachelor botch a batch
of badly baked biscuits?
If the bachelor botched a
batch of badly baked biscuits,
Where are the badly baked
biscuits the bachelor botched?

Betty Botter bought a bit of butter.
"But," said she, "this butter's bitter.
If I put it in my batter,
it will make my batter bitter.
But a bit of better butter—
That would make my batter better."
So Betty Botter bought a
bit of better butter
(better than her bitter butter)
and made her bitter batter
a bit better.

I bought a bit of baking powder and baked a batch of biscuits. I brought a big basket of biscuits back to the bakery and baked a basket of big biscuits.

Then I took the big basket of biscuits and the basket of big biscuits and mixed the big biscuits with the basket of biscuits that was next to the big basket and put a bunch of biscuits from the basket into a biscuit mixer and brought the basket of biscuits and the box of mixed biscuits and the biscuit mixer to the bakery—and opened a can of sardines.

Byron's butler bought Byron's brother butter.

Bess's pet pestered Fess.
Bess's pet pestered Fess.
Bess's pet pestered Fess.

Bernie's thirty dirty turtles
dirtied Ernie.

Bennie bought a bright brown
blouse for Bonnie, but Bonnie
believed Bennie bought a
better bright blue blouse for Betty.

Big pigs in a big pig pen.

Brownie Birdie was a bully.
Brownie's bossy brother Billy
Birdie was a bigger bully.
Brownie and Billy stayed busy
by bullying their buddies. Both
Birdie brothers were big, bad bullies.

TIME CHALLENGE

*How many times can you
say this in 10 seconds?*

Brown, black, blue.

Bill built a big brick building.
Bill built a big brick building.
Bill built a big brick building.

Bridget builds bigger bridges than
Barbara, but the bridges Barbara builds
are better than the bridges Bridget
builds.

The fuzzy bee buzzed the
buzzy busy beehive.

The bumblebees' buzzing didn't
bother the beavers nor did the
beavers' building bother the bumblebees.

Bruce's bird is perched on the broken birch branch.

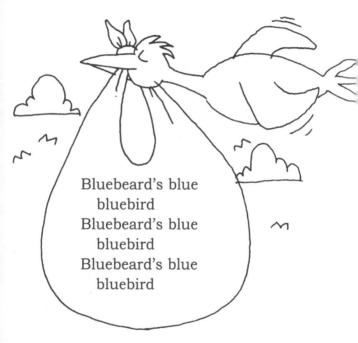

Bluebeard's blue
bluebird
Bluebeard's blue
bluebird
Bluebeard's blue
bluebird

Bluebirds in blue birdbaths.

A batter, a banana, and a bandanna.
A batter, a banana, and a bandanna.
A batter, a banana, and a bandanna.

Both bowlers bought
blue bowling balls,
but both bowled better
with black bowling balls.

Bulb-bowls
Bulb-bowls
Bulb-bowls

The bleak breeze blights the
brightly blooming blossom.

Bright bloom the blossoms on
the brook's bare brown banks.

Bob's blue blobs.
Bob's blue blobs.
Bob's blue blobs.

Blue beads in a blue rattle
rattle blue beads.

Biff Brown bluffed and blustered.

Brad brought Barney's bright
brass bike back.

Buster broke broncos. Buster was
a bronco buster.

"Did you bust the butcher's
  buzzer, Buster?"
"You bet I busted the buzzer,"
  Buster boasted.

❋

I'll bet Beth's beau Brett brought
  Beth both bikes.

❋

The bootblack brought the black
  boot back.

❋

Blair's blue boots are beauties.

❋

A big blue bucket of blue
  blackberries.

❋

Billy's big black-and-blue blister bled.

Biff Brown split bricks.

Blake broke both black bricks, but
brought both brown bricks
Britt borrowed.

The best breath test
tests breath better.

Black bug's blood.
Black bug's blood.
Black bug's blood.

Red bug's blood, bed bug's blood.
Red bug's blood, bed bug's blood.
Red bug's blood, bed bug's blood.

I have a black-backed bath brush.
Do you have a black-backed bath brush?

Beth bathed in both baths.

Pass the big black blank bank book.
If you won't pass the big black
blank bank book back,
then pass the small brown
blank bank book back.

The brave bloke blocked the broken back bank door.

The boy blinked at the blank bank blackboard.

Bland Bea blinks back.
Bland Bea blinks back.
Bland Bea blinks back.

Betty's betting big.

Bill had a billboard.
Bill also had a board bill.
The board bill bored Bill,
So Bill sold his billboard
And paid his board bill.
Then the board bill
No longer bored Bill,
But though he had no board bill,
Neither did he have his billboard.

Three blind mice blew bugles.

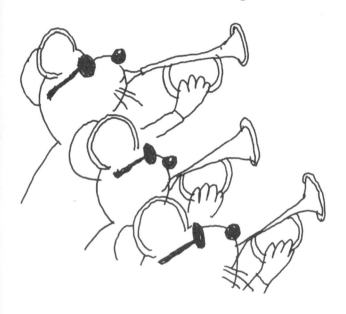

Bring Beverly a bubbling,
bubbling beverage.

Borrowed burros bring borrowed barrels.

Bertha blocked the bleached
back beach benches.

Bob bought a bleached blue-beaded
blazer.

Bess is the best backward blue-blowing
bugler in the Boston brass band.

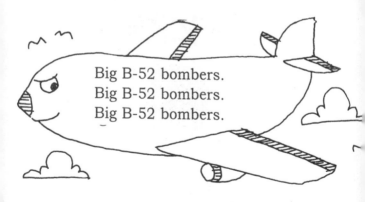

Big B-52 bombers.
Big B-52 bombers.
Big B-52 bombers.

The blunt back blade is bad.

Ted Blake's back brake-block
  broke a bearing.
Did Ted Blake's back brake-block
  break a bearing?
If Ted Blake's back brake-block
  broke a bearing,
Where's the bearing Ted Blake's
  back brake-block broke?

A big black bat flew past.
A big brown bat flew past.
Did the big black bat fly past
faster than the big brown bat
  flew past?

A bitter biting bittern
Bit a better brother bittern,
And the better bittern bit
   the Bitter biter back.
And the bittern, bitten
By the better biting bittern,
Said, "I'm a bitten, bitter, biting,
   bittern, bitten better now, alack!"

Clean clams crammed in clean cans.

Cheap sausage stew.

A canner exceedingly canny,
One morning remarked to his granny,
   "A canner can can
   Anything that he can,
But a canner can't can a can, can he?"

Catch a can canner canning a can
as he does the cancan,
and you've caught a can-canning
can-canning can canner!

Cuthbert's cufflinks.
Cuthbert's cufflinks.
Cuthbert's cufflinks.

A cheeky chimp chucked cheap chocolate chips in the cheap chocolate chip shop.

A chapped chap chopped chips.

The fish-and-chip shop's chips
   are soft chips.

Does this shop stock cheap checkers?

Where can I find a cheerful cheap
   chop suey shop?

Top chopstick shops stock top chopsticks.

Cheerful Charlie chose
  a cheesy chowder.
Did cheerful Charlie choose
  a cheesy chowder?
If cheerful Charlie chose
  a cheesy chowder,
How cheerful was Charlie after he chose
  the cheesy chowder?

Chris criss-crossed the pie crust.

Caleb grabbed clicking crab claws.

Choice chilled cherries cheer Cheryl.

Clarence claims clams can't clap.

Tricky crickets.
Tricky crickets.
Tricky crickets.

Aunt Connie could'a caught an anaconda, but the anaconda caught Aunt Connie.

Had the anaconda been the kind of anaconda that was kinder, that anaconda could'a kissed Aunt Connie.

But the anaconda that caught Aunt Connie was the kind of anaconda that couldn't kiss, so it consumed Aunt Connie.

Crisp crust crackles.
Crisp crust crackles.
Crisp crust crackles.

A cupcake cook in a cupcake cook's cap
cooks cupcakes.

The cute cookie cutters cut cute cookies.
Did the cute cookie cutters
  cut cute cookies?
If the cute cookie cutters
  cut cuter cookies,
Where are the cute cookies
  the cute cookie cutter cut?

Clyde Crow cries quietly.

TIME CHALLENGE

How many times can you say this in 10 seconds?

Crisp cracker crumbs.

Corinne quit cooking quiche because she couldn't quite cook quiche correctly.

If Sue chews shoes, should she choose to chew new shoes or old shoes?

All I want is a proper cup of coffee,
Made in a proper copper coffeepot.
You can believe it or not—
I want a cup of coffee
In a proper coffeepot.
Tin coffeepots or Iron coffeepots,
They're no use to me.
If I can't have a
Proper cup of coffee
In a proper copper coffeepot—
I'll have a cup of tea!

Cooper cut Culver's copper-colored clover.

Chester shucked the chestnuts and
Chuck chucked the shucks.
Did Chester shuck the chestnuts faster
than Chuck chucked the shucks?
Or did Chuck chuck the shucks faster
than Chester shucked the chestnuts?

Cinnamon aluminum linoleum.
Cinnamon aluminum linoleum.
Cinnamon aluminum linoleum.

If a good cook could cook cuckoos so fine,
And a good cook could cook cuckoos
    all the time,
How many cuckoos could a good cook cook
If a good cook could cook cuckoos?

Choppers chop. Droppers drop.
Shoppers shop.

Carol carefully carried Cora's carrots.

✳

The chief Chief chewed the cheap cheese.

✳

New cheese, blue cheese, chew cheese
please.

✳

The class cleaned the cream cheese
churners carefully.

✳

Cora Clinger's coolers were cool,
but Carla Clinger's coolers
were clearly the coolest coolers.

✳

Colin's cooler can't cool
Craig's colas.

A clan of cool crows clings
   close in cold climates.

What could have caused
   the crows to caw?
I think the cars were the cause
   of the crows' cawing.

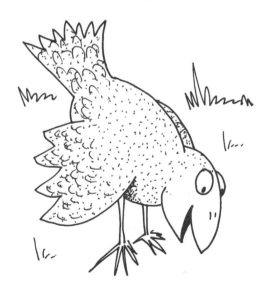

TIME CHALLENGE

*How many times can you
say this in 10 seconds?*

Jerry chewed two chewy cherries.

Kookie cookies.
Kookie cookies.
Kookie cookies.

How much caramel can a canny cannibal cram in a camel, if a canny cannibal can cram caramel in a camel?

Camels can't keep carpets and closets clean.

Clara Kaufman carefully cleaned the carpet in her cousin's kids' clothes closet.

Chloe couldn't close the clothes
closet 'cause her clothes were
crammed too close.

Clyde can clean Chloe's clothes,
but can Clyde cram Chloe's clothes
into Chloe's closet?

Carmen is mad at Matt because
she paid Matt money to clean
her muddy car mats.
Matt cleaned Carmen's muddy car
and left Carmen's car mats muddy.
"Clean the muddy car mats, Matt,
not the muddy car," Carmen muttered.

Carol quarreled.
Carol quarreled.
Carol quarreled.

The cop was in the cot copping a catnap.
When the cop caught the cat in the cot
copping a catnap, the cop kicked
the catnapping cat out of the cot.

The chap in the cap clapped
when he captured the cat in the trap.

Clinton's kittens kicked Clinton's chickens. Clinton caught the kicking kittens
in the kitchen.

"Quit kicking those chickens, you
crazy kicking kittens," Clinton commanded.

Charlene keeps the chalk sharp.
As she sharpens the chalk,
the chalk gets short.
So she keeps a "sharp chalk chart"
to show when to change the chalk.

Carl called Claude.
Carl called Claude.
Carl called Claude.

Ann Chan can't chant Chancey's aunt's
chants.

Had the colt had a coat,
the colt couldn't have
caught cold.

The cowardly cowboy cowered as
the courageous cowboy cornered the
cows.

Carl chose Claire's church
chimes carefully.

The commander commanded
the commandoes.
The commander commanded
the commandoes.
The commander commanded
the commandoes.

Chip's ship sank.
Chip's ship sank.
Chip's ship sank.

TIME CHALLENGE

How many times can you say this in 10 seconds?

Chris' craft crashed.

A curious cream-colored cat crept
   into the crypt and crept out again.
Did the curious cream-colored cat
   creep into the crypt and creep out again?
If the curious cream-colored cat
   crept into the crypt and crept out again,
Where's the curious cream-colored cat that
   crept into the crypt and crept out again?

Who checked the chart of the
cud-chewing cow?

If you must cross a coarse cross cow
across a crowded cow crossing,
cross the cross coarse cow across
the crowded cow crossing carefully.

Cheap sheep soup.
Cheap sheep soup.
Cheap sheep soup.

A clipper shipped several clipped sheep.
Were these clipped sheep the clipper
   ship's sheep?
Or just clipped sheep shipped on a
   clipper ship?

Charles chose the chief cheap
   sheep section.

"Cheep-cheep," chirped the cheery chick.

A clean, covered coffee cup cupboard.

As I was dashing down Cutting Hill,
A-cutting through the air,
I saw Charlie Cutting sitting
In Oscar Cutting's chair.
And Oscar Cutting was sitting
cutting Charlie Cutting's hair.

Great crates create great craters,
but great craters create greater craters.

I do like cheap sea trips,
Cheap sea trips on ships.
I like to be on the deep blue sea,
When the ship she rolls and dips.

If you cross a cross across a cross,
Or cross a stick across a stick,
Or cross a stick across a cross,
Or cross a cross across a stick,
Or stick a stick across a stick,
Or stick a cross across a cross,
Or stick a cross across a stick,
Or stick a stick across a cross,
What a waste of time!

When the computer crashed, the class gasped.

The creek creatures croaked quietly.

Can Claire cue Carl's curtain call?

A cricket critic cricked his neck at a critical cricket match.

Curt carved curves.
Curt carved curves.
Curt carved curves.

The chicken checkers ought to check the chickens that the chicken catchers caught.

The captain's cook was a crook 'cause he took the clock locked in the captain's kitchen cupboard.

I would if I could,
If I couldn't, how could I?
I couldn't if I couldn't,
  could I?
Could you if you couldn't,
  could you?

Chuck's job was to chop chips.
Chuck was a chip chopper.
In fact, he was the top chip chopper.
The chips were shipped to the
chip-chopping shop and
Chuck chopped the chips.
The chip-chopping shop also
had a chip checker.
He checked the chips
Chuck chopped.

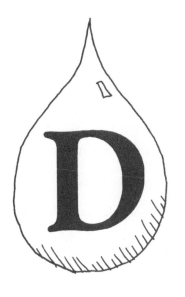

Do drop in
at the
Dewdrop Inn.

How much dew could a dewdrop drop if
a dewdrop did drop dew?

My dame had a lame, tame crane;
My dame had a lame, tame crane.
  Oh, pray, gentle Jane,
  Let my dame's lame crane
Pray drink and come home again.

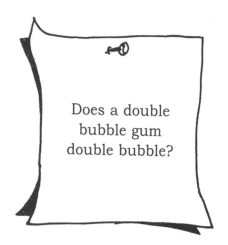

Does a double
bubble gum
double bubble?

Dwayne dwells in drafty dwellings.

The duke dropped the dirty double damask dinner napkin.

Down the deep damp dark dank den.

The deer dined on dough, though the doe dined on dates.

Deer's ears hear clear cheers.

A maid with a duster
  Made a furious bluster
Dusting a bust in the hall.
  When the bust it was dusted,
The bust it was busted,
  The bust it was dust, that's all.

Debbie didn't destroy
Darrell's dishes.
Darrell destroyed
Debbie's dishes.

Disgruntled dishwashers
don't wash dishes.

Jane's drainboard drain just drained
Jane's drainage.

Ducks clucked under the docks.

Drew drew dumb ducks drumming drums.

Ducks don't dunk doughnuts.

Dave's dogs dig deep ditches.

Don't you dare dawdle, Darryl!
Don't you dare dawdle, Darryl!
Don't you dare dawdle, Darryl!

Drew dripped the drink
from the dipper, but he didn't
drink a drop.

When a doctor gets sick and another doctor doctors him, does the doctor doing the doctoring have to doctor the doctor the way the doctor being doctored wants to be doctored, or does the doctor doing the doctoring of the doctor doctor the doctor as he wants to do the doctoring?

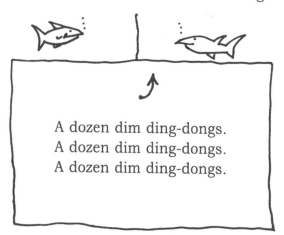

A dozen dim ding-dongs.
A dozen dim ding-dongs.
A dozen dim ding-dongs.

Donna didn't date Darla's daddy's dentists, but Darla did.

The detective effectively
detected the defective device.

The drummers drummed
and the strummers strummed.
The drummers drummed
and the strummers strummed.
The drummers drummed
and the strummers strummed.

Dave's date dared Dave and Dale to dive. Dave didn't dive. "Darn it, Dale, dive!" Dave's date demanded. "Don't dare Dale," Dave declared. "Dale doesn't do dives."

Dan's little delivery to the livery was delayed.

Darby destroyed Dunby's derby.

The dwarf's dwellings are by the dark
wharf. There are dogs by the dark wharf
and they woof at the dwarfs
as the dwarfs walk on the wharf.
When the dark wharf is foggy,
the dwarf's dwellings seem far away
and that makes the dwarfs wary.
That's when the dwarfs wish the dogs

on the dark wharf would woof,
so the dwarves could weave their way
through the fog to their dwellings.
"What are dogs for if not to woof?"
the dwarfs wonder.

Elegant elephants.
Elegant elephants.
Elegant elephants.

Edgar at eight ate eight eggs a day.

Eddie's enemies envied
Eddie's energy.

Esau Wood would saw wood. Oh,
the wood that Wood would saw!
One day Esau Wood saw a saw
saw wood as no other wood-saw
Wood ever saw would saw wood.
Of all the wood-saws Wood ever
saw saw wood, Wood never saw a
wood-saw that would saw like
the wood-saw Wood saw would.
Now Esau saws wood with that
wood-saw he saw saw wood.

*

I saw Esau kissing Kate.
Fact is, we all three saw.
I saw Esau, he saw me,
And she saw I saw Esau.

107

Did you eever iver ever
  in your leaf loaf life
See the deevil divil devil
  kiss his weef wofe wife?
No, I neever niver never
  in my leaf loaf life
Saw the deevil divil devil
  kiss his weef wofe wife.

Ere her ear hears her err,
her ears err here.

Every errant arrow isn't Aaron's
errant arrow.

Ernie yearned to learn to turn urns.

Everett never severed Neville's level.

Exercise instructors instruct struggling exercisers to exercise strongly.

Eloquent elephants telephoned
other eloquent elephants.

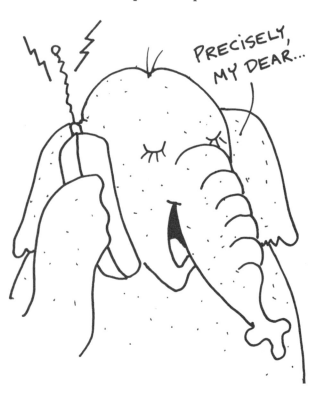

Eleven little leather loafers.
Eleven little leather loafers.
Eleven little leather loafers.

Etta taught her daughter that she ought to barter smarter.

Eight eager eagles ogled old Edgar.

Every errand Randy ran for Erin was in error.

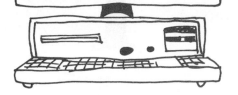

Eighteen apes ate
eighteen apricots.
Eighteen apes ate
eighteen apricots.
Eighteen apes ate
eighteen apricots.

For fine fresh fish, phone Phil.

Frank feasted on flaming fish
at the famous Friday fish fry.

Can a flying fish flee far
from a free fish fry?

Flat flying fish fly faster
than flat, flying fleas.

Free kiwis.
Free kiwis.
Free kiwis.

Fifteen filthy flying foxes.
Fifteen filthy flying foxes.
Fifteen filthy flying foxes.

A fine field of wheat.
A fine field of wheat.
A fine field of wheat.

A fish-sauce shop's sure to sell
fresh fish sauce.

The factory fractured the fragile flask.

Flawless porcelain flasks.
Flawless porcelain flasks.
Flawless porcelain flasks.

Fran feeds fish fresh fish food.

*How many times can you
say this in 10 seconds?*

The fleas fled far from the ferret's fur.

Menu

Fried fresh fish,
Fish fried fresh,
Fresh fried fish.
Fresh fish fried
Or fish fresh fried

118

Friendly Bugs

Friendly fleas and fireflies.
Friendly fleas and fireflies.
Friendly fleas and fireflies.

Friendly fleas and huffy fruit flies.
Friendly fleas and huffy fruit flies.
Friendly fleas and huffy fruit flies.

TIME CHALLENGE

How many times can you say this in 10 seconds?

The fleas fled far from the ferret's fur.

Five fat French fleas freeze.
Five fat French fleas freeze.
Five fat French fleas freeze.

A fly and a flea in a flue
Were imprisoned, so what could they do?
Said the fly, "Let us flee!"
  "Let us fly!" said the flea
And they flew through the flaw in the
  flue.

Said the flea to the fly as he flew
  through the flue,
"There's a flaw in the floor of the flue."
Said the fly to the flea as he flew
  through the flue,
"A flaw in the flue doesn't bother me.
Does it bother you?"

The fruit fly flew through the flute and into the throat of the frightened flutist.

The furry fly flitted from flower to flower.
The furry fly flitted from flower to flower.
The furry fly flitted from flower to flower.

Four fliers flip-flop.
Four fliers flip-flop.
Four fliers flip-flop.

The fickle finger of fate flips fat frogs flat.
The fickle finger of fate flips fat frogs flat.
The fickle finger of fate flips fat frogs flat.

For French shrimp, try a
French shrimp shop.

Fat flat frozen flounders.
Fat flat frozen flounders.
Fat flat frozen flounders.

Freddie's frying five
fresh flying fish.

Fresh figs.
Fresh figs.
Fresh figs.

Frank freed Fred's fast frog.

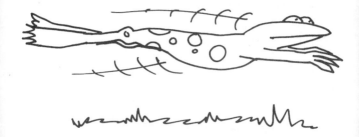

Four fat, flat-footed frogs
flapped their floppy flippers.

Five frantic frogs fled
from fifty fierce fishes.

Five fifers free,
Fifing in the fog,
Phyllis, Fran,
And Phil and Dan
And Philip's funny frog.

Flighty Flo Fisk and frisky Fritz Fisk.

Of all the felt I ever felt
I never felt a piece of felt
That felt the same as that felt felt
When I first felt that felt.

Fine fresh fodder.
Fine fresh fodder.
Fine fresh fodder.

A fat-free fruit float.
A fat-free fruit float.
A fat-free fruit float.

Five flashy flappers
Flitting forth fleetly
Found four flighty flappers
Flirting flippantly.

Few free fruit flies fly from flames.

Free flag.
Free flag.
Free flag.

Fifty-five flags
freely flutter
from the floating
frigate.

Five flags flying from
A flimsy flagpole.

Three fluffy feathers fell from
Phoebe's flimsy fan.

The flood flooded Frank's floor.

Four free-flow pipes flow freely.

Freckle-faced Freddie fidgets.

I'd rather lather Father
Than Father lather me.
When Father lathers
He lathers rather free.

Phillip Fox fixed Phyllis Floyd's fax.

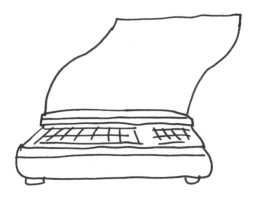

A fly fled fat Flo's flat.
A flea fled fat Flo's flat.
Did the fly or the flea
flee fat Flo's flat first?

Fleming frowned when Fletcher
flung his favorite fossil.

Phil fell four floors face first.

Frank's friend fainted.

Frank faxed the facts in the file folder to his friends in Frankfort.

Phil felt funny folding fifty file folders.

Frank flunked French.

Fifty-five firefighters fried
fifty-five french fries.

I fear this flowered floral
fabric is flawed.

Feed the flies fly food, Floyd!

Farrah's flannel fabric
frequently frays.

A lively young fisher named Fischer
Fished for fish from the edge of a fissure.
   A fish with a grin
   Pulled the fisherman in.
Now they're fishing the fissure for
   Fischer.

Fortunately, Frank Frye's father
fixed the phones.

TIME CHALLENGE

How many times can you say this in 10 seconds?

Fleas fly from fries.

Fran's favorite flowers finally flourished.

Four frightening flashes.
Four frightening flashes.
Four frightening flashes.

Fancy Nancy didn't fancy
    doing fancy work.
But Fancy Nancy's fancy auntie
did fancy Nancy
    doing fancy work.
So Fancy Nancy
    did fancy work for
Fancy Nancy's fancy auntie.

Greek grapes.
Greek grapes.
Greek grapes.

The cruel ghoul cooks gruel.

Gargoyles gargle oil.

TIME CHALLENGE

*How many times can you
say this in 10 seconds?*

Gail grew great grapes.

Granny gave Gary grape gum.

Gus goes by Blue Goose bus.

Granny's gray goose goes last.

Great gray geese graze gaily daily.

Goats and ghosts.
Goats and ghosts.
Goats and ghosts.

Good gunsmoke, bad gunsmoke.
Good gunsmoke, bad gunsmoke.
Good gunsmoke, bad gunsmoke.

Good blood, bad blood.

Gig-whip.
Gig-whip.
Gig-whip.

Cows graze in droves on grass that grows on grooves in groves.

Gale's great glass globe glows green.

The glum groom grew glummer.

Gretchen's guests always get garlic grits. The guests act glad to get the grits, but the guests agree that Gretchen's garlic grits are gross.

Glenda glued Gilda's galoshes.
Glenda glued Gilda's galoshes.
Glenda glued Gilda's galoshes.

Granny Greer greased the gears with green gear grease.

The grumpy guppy grimly grinned.

HE'S SO GRUMPY!

Gophers go golfing

Grant grasped at the grass.

Glen lent Gwen Wayne's wrench.

Gene cleans queens' screens.

Glum Gwendolyn's glasses.
Glum Gwendolyn's glasses.
Glum Gwendolyn's glasses.

Three gray-green greedy geese,
Feeding on a weedy piece,
  The piece was weedy,
  and the geese were greedy,
Three gray-green greedy geese.

Glory grows gladioli.
Glory grows gladioli.
Glory grows gladioli.

Higgledy-Piggledy.
Higgledy-Piggledy.
Higgledy-Piggledy.

The hare's ear heard ere the hare heeded.

PSSSST!

High roller.
Low roller.
Lower a roller.

The hairy hare stares at the
hairier hare, and the hairier hare
stares at the hairiest hare.
Here we have a three-hare stare affair.

Horrible Heidi hears hairy Horace holler.

Hugh chooses huge shoes.

Has Hal's heel healed?
Has Hal's heel healed?
Has Hal's heel healed?

Hurry, Harry!
Hurry, Harry!
Hurry, Harry!

Hillary's hairy hound hardly hurries.

How much hair could a hairnet net,
If a hairnet could net hair?

Hannah had her hair henna'd.
Hannah had her hair henna'd.
Hannah had her hair henna'd.

152

Harry Hunt hunts heavy hairy hares.
Does Harry Hunt hunt heavy hairy hares?
If Harry Hunt hunts heavy hairy hares,
Where are the heavy hairy hares Harry
Hunt hunts?

Hiccup teacup!
Hiccup teacup!
Hiccup teacup!

Heed the head henpecker!

"Hello, Harry Healy!" hollered Holly
Hartley.

If a Hottentot taught
A Hottentot tot,
To talk ere the tot could totter,
Ought the Hottentot tot
Be taught to say "ought,"
Or what ought to be taught her?

If to hoot and to toot
A Hottentot tot
Was taught by a Hottentot tutor,
Should the tutor get hot
If the Hottentot tot
Hoots and toots at the Hottentot tutor?

A hard-hearted shorn honker
honked his horned horn hatefully.

Harry helped Herman herd
a herd of Herefords.

TIME CHALLENGE

How many times can you say this in 10 seconds?

Horse hairs are coarse
hairs, of course.

Harlan hid from the hornets
he heard humming in the
hollow hornet tree.

In Huron a hewer, Hugh Hughes,
Hewed yews of unusual hues.
Hugh Hughes used blue yews
To build sheds for new ewes;
So his new ewes blue-hued ewe-sheds use.

How hollow Helen Hull hobbles on hills!

A haddock!
A haddock!
A black-spotted haddock!
A black spot
On the black back
Of a black-spotted haddock!

Old Howell owned a house on which
old owls howled.

Ike ships ice chips in ice chips ships.

Can you imagine an imaginary menagerie manager imagining managing an imaginary menagerie?

Isis envies Isley's ivy.

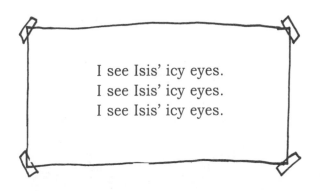

I see Isis' icy eyes.
I see Isis' icy eyes.
I see Isis' icy eyes.

Indianapolis isn't in India, Andy.
Indians are in India and Indians
are in Indiana. But the Indian Indians
and the Indiana Indians aren't identical
Indians. The Indians in India are Indian
Indians, and the Indians in Indiana are
indigenous Indians.

Ira acquired iron awnings.

Insects. Six insects. Six sick insects.

Isn't Isadora adorable?

Iggy is interested in visiting with Izzy, but Izzy isn't interested in visiting with Iggy. Even so, in this instance, Izzy isn't even in, so Izzy couldn't visit with Iggy even if Izzy was interested, which he isn't.

There is pie in my eye.
Will I cry? Will I die?
Though I'm shy, I won't lie.
It might cause a sty,
but I deny that I'll die
or cry from the pie in my eye.

Inconsiderate intruders introduce
other inconsiderate intruders.

I'll lie idle on the isle.

Our Joe wants to know if your Joe
will lend our Joe your Joe's banjo.
If your Joe won't lend our Joe
your Joe's banjo, our Joe won't lend
your Joe our Joe's banjo
when our Joe has a banjo!

Joe's giraffe juggled jelly jars.
Jack's giraffe juggled jam jars.

June sheep sleep soundly.

Are those jesters joking or are
those jesters jousting?

Jules the jeweler generally chooses
Jewel's jewelry.

James the jailer changed the
jail's chairs and chained the
chairs to the jail.

A gentle judge judges justly.
A gentle judge judges justly.
A gentle judge judges justly.

James jostled Jean while Jean jostled
Joan.

Jim jogs in the gym.
Jane jogs in the jungle.

Kinky kite kits.
Kinky kite kits.
Kinky kite kits.

171

Nutty Knott was not in.
Nutty Knott was out,
Knotting knots in netting.
Nutty Knott was out,
But lots of nots
Were in Nutty Knott's knotty netting.

Come kick six sticks quick.

Keep clean socks in a clean sock stack.

> Knee deep, deep knee.
> Knee deep, deep knee.
> Knee deep, deep knee.

TIME CHALLENGE

How many times can you say this in 10 seconds?

Kirk's starched shirts.

Keenly cleaning copper kettles.
Keenly cleaning copper kettles.
Keenly cleaning copper kettles.

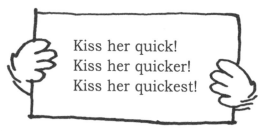

Kiss her quick!
Kiss her quicker!
Kiss her quickest!

King Kong plays Ping-Pong.

Kayaking keeps Katherine's kangaroo
calm, but Katherine's kangaroo
can't kayak in Kansas,
so Katherine carts her kangaroo
to Kentucky where
her kangaroo can kayak quietly.

The knight's
wife knit the
knight
new knickers.

A knapsack strap.
A knapsack strap.
A knapsack strap.

A lump of red leather
A red leather lump.

✳

Lily Little lit a little lamp.
Lily Little lit a little lamp.
Lily Little lit a little lamp.

✳

Little Ida lied a little.
Little Ida lied a lot.

✳

Red Leather!
Yellow leather!

✳

Larry's lair lacks locks.

Lonely lowland llamas are ladylike.

Lanky Lawrence lost his lass
  and lobster.
Did Lanky Lawrence lose his lass
  and lobster?
If Lanky Lawrence lost his lass
  and lobster,
Where's the lass and lobster
  Lanky Lawrence lost?

Lee loves to rob lobsters.

Let lame lambs live.
Let lame lambs live.
Let lame lambs live.

Lizzie's dizzy lizard didn't litter Lizzie's lot.

Local loggers' lawyers.

Larry sent the latter a letter later.

Literally literary.
Literally literary.
Literally literary.

Lester lists the lesser lesson last.

Lesser leather never weathered
lesser wetter weather.

Lemon-lime liniment.
Lemon-lime liniment.
Lemon-lime liniment.

Little licorice lollipops.
Little licorice lollipops.
Little licorice lollipops.

Lisa laughed listlessly.

Luke likes licorice.
Luke likes licorice.
Luke likes licorice.

TIME CHALLENGE

*How many times can you say this in
10 seconds?*

Loose loops.

The less the lame loon
leaned on its little lame leg,
the less the loon limped.

Luminous aluminum.
Luminous aluminum.
Luminous aluminum.

TIME CHALLENGE

*How many times can you
say this in 10 seconds?*

Long lush lashes.

Levi left the leaves lying
on the littered lawn.

Lon Longman loaded a lotta
    long logs.
If Long Longman loaded a lotta
    long logs,
then where are all the long logs
    Lon Longman loaded?

Libby locked Larry in the lobby.
"Mom! Libby locked me in the lobby,"
   Larry lamented.
"Let Larry loose, Libby,"
   Mom laughed.

The llama loaned the lamb
   a long ladder.
The lamb loaned the llama
   a little lamp.

He who laughs last laughs last.

Mummies munch much mush;
Monsters munch much mush;
Many mummies and monsters
Must munch much mush.

190

Michael's mouse munched muffins.

A missing mixture measure.
A missing mixture measure.
A missing mixture measure.

The minx mixed a medicine mixture.

Moses supposes his toeses are roses;
But Moses supposes erroneously;
For nobody's toeses are poses of roses
As Moses supposes his toeses to be.

Mr. Melton made a metal motor.
Mr. Melton made a metal motor.
Mr. Melton made a metal motor.

Mussels with mustard is Mister
Mussman's main meal.

Mister Mitter admitted that he
missed Mrs. Mitter.

Miss Smith lisps as she talks
and lists as she walks.

"Are you aluminiuming, my man?"
"No, I'm copperbottoming 'em, mum."

Mark's name makes Nate's
namesake shake.

I miss my Swiss Miss.
My Swiss Miss misses me.

Much mashed mushrooms.
Much mashed mushrooms.
Much mashed mushrooms.

A mermaid made Mike marmalade.

Matt's mismatched mittens
make Matt miserable.

The monster's mother made many morsels
for the monster to munch.
Most of the morsels the monster's
mother made were moist,
but the most moist morsels
were mainly the morsels that
the monster munched.
"My, my," the monster's mother murmured.
"My little monster may have made
a mistake. Too many moist morsels
may make you miserable."

Nick knits Nixon's knickers.

Nellie's new knitting needles knit neatly.

198

Nineteen nice knights.
Nineteen nice knights.
Nineteen nice knights.

TIME CHALLENGE

How many times can you say this in 10 seconds?

No one knows Wayne.

I need not your needles,
They're needless to me,
For the needing of needles
Is needless, you see.
But did my neat trousers
But need to be kneed,
I then should have need
Of your needles indeed.

200

Nine nimble noblemen nibbled nuts.

Nicholas noticed a nick on
Nicollette's necklace.

Nippy Noodle nipped his
  neighbor's nutmegs.
Did Nippy Noddle nip his
  neighbor's nutmegs?
If Nippy Noodle nipped his
  neighbor's nutmegs,
Where are the neighbor's nutmegs
  Nippy Noodle nipped?

Nine nice night nymphs.
Nine nice night nymphs.
Nine nice night nymphs.

Nina never knew her neighbor Noah knew her.

Ned Nott was shot
  and Sam Shott was not.
So it's better to be Shott than Nott.
Some say Nott was not shot,
  but Shott swears he shot Nott.
Either the shot Shott shot at Nott
  was not shot,
  or Nott was shot.
But if the shot Shott shot
  shot Shott himself,
Then Shott would be shot
  and Nott would not.
However, the shot Shott shot
  shot not Shott but Nott.
It's not easy to say who was shot
  and who was not.
But we know who was Shott
  and who was Nott.

Norse myths.
Norse myths.
Norse myths.

There's no need to light a night light
On a light night like tonight;
For a night light's just a slight light,
On a light night like tonight.

Nancy naps at noon and
Nick knows it's not nice to knock
when Nancy's napping.

205

Knit this net with neat knots.
Knots that are not neat
are not the knots this net needs.

Ninety-nine knitted knick-knacks
were nicked by ninety-nine knitted
knick-knack nickers.

"Nighty-night, knight," said one knight to the other knight the other night. "Ninety night, knight," answered the other knight the other night.

One worm wiggled
  while
Two tiny toads tasted tea
  while
Three thirsty turkeys thought
  while
Four frantic flamingoes flapped
  while
Five ferocious felines flashed their fangs
  while
Six slow sloths silently slept
  while
Seven stinky skunks started singing
  while
Eight elderly elks eloped
  while
Nine needlefish knitted napkins
  while
Ten tarantulas tapped tambourines.

Old oily corks.

"Under the mother otter,"
uttered the other otter.

Awful old Ollie oils oily autos.

The owner of the Inside Inn
Was outside his Inside Inn
With his inside outside his Inside Inn.

Oliver Oglethorpe ogled
   an owl and oyster.
Did Oliver Oglethorpe ogle
   an owl and oyster?
If Oliver Oglethorpe ogled
   an owl and oyster,
Where's the owl and oyster
   Oliver Oglethorpe ogled?

Orville ordered ordinary ornaments.

An oyster met an oyster,
And they were oysters two;
Two oysters met two oysters,
And they were oysters too;
Four oysters met a pint of milk,
And they were oyster stew.

Peter Piper picked a peck
  of pickled pepper,
A peck of pickled peppers
  Peter Piper picked.
If Peter Piper picked a peck
  of pickled peppers,
Where's the peck of pickled peppers
  Peter Piper picked?

The perky parrot playfully pecked
the pirate's pate.

Pairs of parakeets parent
parrots perfectly.

The playful purple parrot pecked
the pink parrot's plume.

Pass the pink peas please

＊

Plain bun, plum bun.
Plain bun, plum bun.
Plain bun, plum bun.

＊

Please prune plum trees promptly.

＊

The plum pickers plucked
the plump plums.
The plum pickers plucked
the plump plums.
The plum pickers plucked
the plump plums.

＊

Pat, please pass Patsy's plum party
patties.

A panda playing with paper
placed her paw on a
piece of parchment and
promptly produced a paw print.

Peter Potter splattered a plate of peas on Patty Platt's pink plaid pants.

Phyllis Bickle spilled Bill Spector's sack of speckled pickles.

TIME
CHALLENGE

*How many times can you
say this in 10 seconds?*

Penny penned a pretty poem.

ROSES
ARE RED.
VIOLETS
ARE
BLUE...

Patty probably purchased
plenty pretty party paper.

220

Polly painted a plate of pasta
on Peter's pizza parlor poster.

Peter Piper paid for pepperoni pizza.
If Peter Piper paid for pepperoni pizza,
Then where's the pepperoni pizza
Peter Piper purchased?

Peter poked a poker at the piper,
so the piper poked pepper at Peter.

Paul, please pause for proper applause.

A peck of pesky pixies.
A peck of pesky pixies.
A peck of pesky pixies.

Picky pickpockets pick picked pockets.

Pop bottles pop-bottles
  in pop shops;
The pop-bottles Pop bottles
  poor Pop drops.
When Pop drops pop-bottles,
  pop-bottles plop;
When pop-bottles topple,
  Pop mops slop.

Painters
Planters
Pointers

Please place the pleated pressed pants on the plain pressing plank.

Preshrunk skirts.
Preshrunk skirts.
Preshrunk skirts.

Please, Pam, put proper pleats in Pete's pants.

Pastor Craster can plaster casts faster than the last pastor.

Pat pet Peg's pig.

Peg's parrot pecked Pat,
Peg's pets, the pig, and the parrot.

Paul put a pound of pretzels
in a purple paper pouch.

Peggy Babcock's mummy.
Peggy Babcock's mummy.
Peggy Babcock's mummy.

Pretty precious plants.

TIME CHALLENGE

How many times can you say this in 10 seconds?

Polly planted potted plants.

Poor pure Pierre.
Poor pure Pierre.
Poor pure Pierre.

Please prepare the paired pared pears
near the unprepared pears near the pool.

Pop's popcorn popper probably
popped the popcorn properly.

Preston's probably polishing
Peter's pretty pewter pots.
People pay pros for playing.

227

People pay pros for playing.

Peter's plane is plainly painted.
Peter is paid plenty to paint planes.

Mr. Pletcher paints Mrs. Pitcher
pictures of peaches.

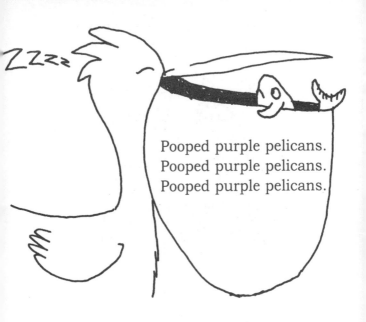

Pooped purple pelicans.
Pooped purple pelicans.
Pooped purple pelicans.

Pick a purple pocket.
Pick a purple pocket.
Pick a purple pocket.

Is a pleasant peasant's pheasant present?

The prince pinched the princess,
so the princess pinched the prince.

Pale pink plumage.
Pale pink plumage.
Pale pink plumage.

Matt batted, Patty putted and
Pepe punted.
Then Patty batted, Pepe putted, and
Matt punted.
Then Pepe batted, Matt putted, and
Patty punted.

When platters shatter, scatter.
They splatter matter.

Pretty poor peace prospects.

233

The quack quit asking quick questions.

The queen coined quick clipped quips.

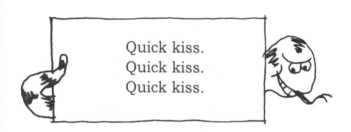

Quick kiss.
Quick kiss.
Quick kiss.

Quakes cause cracks.

Quincey! Quack quietly or quit quacking!

A right-handed fellow named Wright,
In writing "write" always wrote "rite"
  Where he meant to write right.
  If he'd written "write" right,
Wright would not have wrought rot
  writing "rite."

235

TIME CHALLENGE

*How many times can you
say this in 10 seconds?*

A well-read redhead.

Rita repeated what Reardon recited
when Reardon read the remarks.

The renter refused to remit the rent
until a roofer removed the rotten wood
from the rotten roof.

Russ removes rust from wristwatches.
He's Russ, the wristwatch rust remover.

The right rear wheel on
Willy's rally racer
won't roll well.

Ray's runway runs one way.

Rhoda raised red roses.
Wanda raised white roses.

Richard whined when his wet
wristwatch rusted.

TIME CHALLENGE

How many times can you say this in 10 seconds?

Rigid wicker rockers.

Remove the raw rice. Once the raw rice
is removed, roast the white rice.

Reed rode in the red wagon
when he went to Reagan's.
Reed's road was rough,
so Reed refused a return ride
in the red wagon.

Rival river runners rode the wild river.

Round and round the rugged rocks
the ragged rascal ran.

Rex wrecks wet rocks.

Robin robs wealthy widows.

If rustlers wrestle wrestlers,
While rustlers rustle rustlers,
Could rustlers rustle wrestlers
While wrestlers wrestle rustlers?

The rhino wore
a white ribbon.
The white ribbon is
what the rhino wore.

Really rich roaches wear wristwatches.

Rough rural roads.
Rough rural roads.
Rough rural roads.

Ronald won't roll around
the round roller rink.

Ruth rowed as Roth rode in the rowboat.
Roth refused to row. It was rude of Roth
to ride without rowing, while Ruth
rowed as she rode with Roth.

TIME CHALLENGE

How many times can you say this in 10 seconds?

The right fruit is ripe fruit.

Raise Ruth's red roof.
Raise Ruth's red roof.
Raise Ruth's red roof.

Rush the washing, Russell!

Really rotten writing.

TIME CHALLENGE

How many times can you say this in 10 seconds?

Rich, ripe, red, raw raisins.

Ron won't run while Wayne runs.
Why won't Ron run while Wayne runs?
Wayne ruined Ron's new Reboks.
"Wayne's to blame," claims Ron.

Reverend Welch recommended
wide record racks.

Rudolf resented Ryan's relentless rudeness.

Ray's wife raised rice.
The rice Ray's wife raised
was wild rice.

Red wrens' wings.
Red wrens' wings.
Red wrens' wings.

Real rear wheels.
Real rear wheels.
Real rear wheels.

Six small slick seals.
Six small slick seals.
Six small slick seals.

Seth's sharp spacesuit shrank.

"Stay seated, Stephanie,"
Stephen said.

Sherman shops at cheap chop suey shops.

Mrs. Smith's Fish Sauce Shop.

Is Sherry's shortcake shop shut?
Is Shelly's shortstop shop shut?

She sells Swiss sweets.

Six crisp snacks.
Six crisp snacks.
Six crisp snacks.

Sneers and snarls and snail snips.

Stacey Street tasted the tasty treats.
The treats tasted tasty to Stacey.

Are the soup and stew through?
The soup's through,
but the stew's glue.

Sixteen slim, silky slippers.
Sixteen slim, silky slippers.
Sixteen slim, silky slippers.

Something stinks and I think
what stinks are the things
in the sink.

YUK!

Sheila seldom sells shelled shrimps.

She sells seashells by the seashore.

Selfish sharks sell shut shellfish.

Spicy fish sauce.

Stacks of salty snacks
make Sam slurp and smack.

Spike spilled the special sauce.

The stinky socks are soaking
   in the soap in the sink.
If the socks still stink after soaking,
   sit them in the steamer.
After soaking and steaming,
   the stinky socks should smell super.

Stanley Steele still thinks someone stole
his smooth steel sling shot.

Sally Stiller saddled six sorrel stallions.

Silly Sally's slick saddle seldom seemed soft. Still, Sally sat sidesaddle and slowly sidled off.

Susie's shirt shop sells preshrunk shirts.

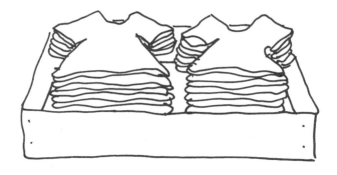

Slick silk.
Slick silk.
Slick silk.

Sharon sews shocking shirts for soldiers.

The sad soldier should shoot soon.

Sharpshooters should shoot slowly.

Soldiers' shoulders shudder
when shrill shells shriek.

Should six shaking soldiers share the
shattered shield?

The short soldier shoots straight.

258

Sixty-six sick six-shooters.

Stagecoach stops.
Stagecoach stops.
Stagecoach stops.

*How many times can you
say this in 10 seconds?*

Soft, smooth snake skin.

The spunky skunk slumped
  and the stinky slug slouched.
Soon they switched and
  the spunky skunk slouched
  and the stinky slug slumped.

Small, smart snakes smelling
smoked steaks.

How many slim, slimy snakes
would slither silently to the sea
if slim, slimy snakes
could slither silently?

"Shoot, Sally!" shouted Slim Sam.

Stu's shoe was in Sue's stew.

Are Stan's scuffed snowshoes
stuck in the snowy slush?

Sue saw Sam Sawyer
sawing cedar shavings.
Sue said, "Stop sawing, Sam,"
and Sam Sawyer stopped.

Mr. See and Mr. Soar were old friends.
See owned a saw and
Soar owned a seesaw.
Now See's saw sawed Soar's seesaw
before Soar saw See,
which made Soar sore.
Had Soar seen See's saw
before See saw Soar's seesaw,
then See's saw would not have sawed
Soar's seesaw.
But See saw Soar's seesaw
before Soar saw See's saw,
so See's saw sawed Soar's seesaw.
It was a shame to let See
see Soar so sore,
because See's saw sawed
Soar's seesaw.

No shipshape ships shop
stocks shop-soiled shirts.

"Sure the ship's ship-shape, sir!"

Shallow sailing ships
should shun shallow shoals.

The shallow ship showed signs of sinking.

The ship's ceiling was
so soaked and soiled,
the sailor had to seal
the soiled ceiling with ceiling sealer.

Sixty-four swift sloops swing shorewards.

The sea ceaseth seething.
The sea ceaseth seething.
The sea ceaseth seething.

HEE
HEE

Smelts

Of all the smells I ever smelt,
I never smelt a smell that smelt
Like that smell I smelt smelled.

A selfish shellfish smelt a stale fish.
If the stale fish was a smelt,
Then the selfish shellfish smelt a
smelt.

Should a shad selling shrimps for a shark,
Cease to shuck the shamed shrimps,
   who remark,
   "Serve us not without dressing!
   'Tis really distressing!"
Or should he just shuck the shrimps
   in the dark?

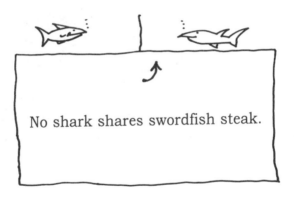

No shark shares swordfish steak.

Steffie strained stew
through the soup strainer.

"Swim, Sam, swim,
Show them you're a swimmer!
Six sharp sharks seek small snacks,
So swim, Sam, swim!

Swan swam over the sea.
"Swim, Swan, Swim!"
Swan swam back again;
"Well swum, Swan!"

Some say shy shippers ship shy sheep.

✳

Six sly shavers sheared six shy sheep.

✳

Shameless shepherds shampoo shy sheep.

Six sick shorn sheep.

The sixth sheik's sixth sheep's sick.

Shorn sheep shouldn't sleep in a shack.
Shorn sheep should sleep in a shed.

The shady shoe shop shows
sharp sharkskin shoes.

Sharp sharkskin shoes.
Sharp sharkskin shoes.
Sharp sharkskin shoes.

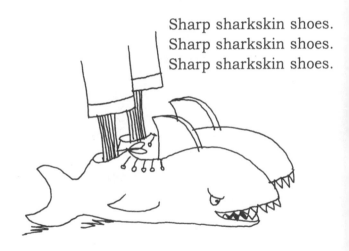

Sid's shabby silver shoes
still shine.

Sooty Sukey
  Shook some soot
From sister Susie's
  Sooty shoes.

The shrewd shrew's suede shoes.

Steph's stock of stacked
soccer socks stinks.

Shoes and socks
  shock Susan.

The suitor wore shorts and a short
  shooting suit to a short shoot.
But the shorts didn't suit
  the short shooting suit,
And at the short shoot,
  the short shooting suit didn't suit.
Oh, shoot!

Six snakes sniffed six sticks.
The snakes sniffed so softly
that their sniffing seemed silent.
Soon their soft sniffing stopped.
Then the six snakes
that sniffed the six sticks
simply slithered away.

I went into my garden to slay snails.
I saw my little sister slaying snails.
I said, "Hello, my little sister,
are you slaying snails?
If you slay snails, please slay small snails."

Sal's sign said, "Small snails for sale."
"Sal's small snails smell stale," Sid said.

Sally Swim saw Sadie Slee
Slowly, sadly swinging.
"She seems sorrowful," said she.
So she started singing.
Sadie smiled, soon swiftly swung;
Sitting straight, steered swiftly.
"See," said Sally, "something sung
Scatters sunshine swiftly!"

Surely the sun shall shine soon.

Some shun summer sunshine.

Shirley Simms shrewdly shuns
sunshine and sleet.

Sally studied stenciling.

Stupid Stanley Sands
stifled Steven Stubbs.

Sue sucks sugar and sherbet
through a straw.

Sixty shifty shoplifters
shoplifting on a nifty ship.

The sun shines on the shop signs.

Shabby soldiers shovel
soft snow slowly.

Sneak-thieves seized the skis.

Sloppy skiers slide on slick ski slopes.

Sleepy Joe of snowy Stowe
Slid swiftly into action.
    Aboard his sled
    Away he sped,
He's sleeping now, in traction.

Seven sleek
sleepless sleepers
seek sleep.

The slightly sloping shed slips.

The shaky shed sheds sheets of shale.

Sick cattle slip on slick ski slopes.

If he slipped, should she slip?

Is there a strap on the cap
  on the chap?
Or is there no strap on the cap
  on the chap?

Sloppy shortstops.
Sloppy shortstops.
Sloppy shortstops.

Sixty-six sticky skeletons.
Sixty-six sticky skeletons.
Sixty-six sticky skeletons.

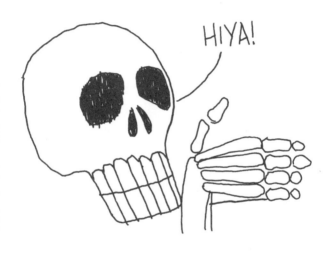

The sly sheet slasher slashed sheets.

She shall sew a slit sheet shut.

A ghost's sheets would soon shrink
in such suds.

HIYA!

She shrieks as she stitches sheets.

Should she sell sheer sheets
or should she sell shaggy shawls?

Amidst the mists and coldest frosts,
With barest wrists and stoutest boasts,
He thrusts his fists against the posts,
And still insists he sees the ghosts.

Some say Seymour saw more,
　　but Seymour won't say more.
"Saw what you saw, Seymour!"
　　some shouted.

Sally sells soil samples
　　at the soil store.
Sometimes there are seashells
　　in the soil samples Sally sells.

"Go, my son, and shut the shutter."
This I heard a mother mutter.
"Shutter's shut," the boy did mutter,
"I can't shut'er any shutter."

Should she shut summer shutters slowly
or should she shut summer shutters
swiftly?

It is so chilly, the silly child
should soon shut the shutters.

Steven Stanley sees seven stars.

Does someone know a synonym
  for cinnamon?
Someone once said that cinnamon
  has no synonym.
But surely there must be a synonym
  for cinnamon.

286

Shouldn't sweet-scented shaving soap
  soothe sore skin?

If silly Sally will shilly-shally,
  shall silly Willy willy-nilly
  shilly-shally, too?

A skunk sat on a stump.
The skunk thunk the stump stunk,
But the stump thunk the skunk stunk.

Sad skunk.
Sad skunk.
Sad skunk.

Shawn shaves a short cedar shingle thin.

Should Shawn shave a short, thin,
   single cedar shingle thin,
or shave a short, thin,
   single, cedar shingle thinner?

I had an old saw,
And I bought a new saw.
I took the handle off the sold saw
And put it on the new saw.
And of all the saws
I ever saw,
I never saw a saw saw
Like that new saw sawed.

Some slow sloths sleep soundly.
Some slow sloths snore strongly.

TIME CHALLENGE

*How many times can you
say this in 10 seconds?*

Sissy saw some simple thimbles.

Shirley showed Cher
some chairs she sewed.

Sid's sister assisted Sissy.

Sharon sewed six shiny suits.

Suzie's sister saw some scissors
Suzie set on her sofa.

Mr. Spink thinks the sphinx stinks.

Scott's skate slipped as Scott skated.
"I think I'll skip these slippery skates,"
Scott said.

Sarah Sawyer sold several soldiers sodas.

Sarah slurped soda through straight, striped soda straws.

Several nervous servers spilled slops.

Several silly servers served Sally squash soup.

Stewart soon stopped sniffing the stinky stuff Sandy stirred with the stick.

Does this shop stock shot silk shorts?

If she stops at the shop where I stop,
and if she shops at the shop where I
  shop,
then I shan't stop at the shop
where she stops to shop.

Showy sashes in a shut sash shop.

Such a shapeless sash!
Such a shapeless sash!
Such a shapeless sash!

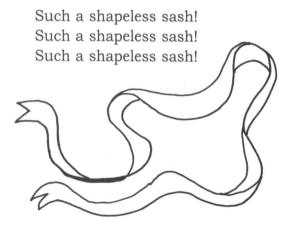

The shepherd swiftly sheared the sleepy sheep with the sharp scissors.

TIME CHALLENGE

*How many times can you
say this in 10 seconds?*

Sue sure seems scared of school.

298

The old school scold
Sold the school coal scuttle;
If the old school scold sold
The school coal scutle,
The school should scold
And scuttle the old school scold.

"What a strange stain," stated Stan.
That stain was the strangest stain
Stan said he'd seen.

Sy's son shines signs and sighs shyly.

Stan stopped stealing Sam's stamps.

Chester Sutter just suggested
Jess test Esther's chess set.

Mrs. Swister kissed her sister's blister.

I snuff shop snuff.
Do you snuff shop
snuff?

Sal served Saul some sour soy sauce.

Sometimes Sheila thinks
such soft thoughts.

Down the slippery slide they slid,
Sitting slightly sideways;
Slipping swiftly, see them skid
On holidays and Fridays.

Scams, stings, and skulduggery.
Scams, stings, and skulduggery.
Scams, stings, and skulduggery.

Through rifts in the lofts,
The soft snow sifts.
Then the white sheet lifts
And the wind packs drifts.

"Stow your snowshoes, Sue."

A tutor who tooted a flute
Tried to tutor two tooters to toot.
Said the two to the tutor,
"Is it harder to toot
Or to tutor two tooters to toot?"

Timothy tapped on the tympani.

I thought a thought
But the thought I thought I thought
    wasn't the thought I thought.
If the thought I thought
    had been the thought
    I thought I thought,
I wouldn't have thought so much.

Do thick tinkers think?

There goes one tough top cop!
There goes one tough top cop!
There goes one tough top cop!

Tea for the thin twin tinsmith.

That's Tim's stack of tin thumbtacks.

Thick ticks think thin ticks are sick.

The throne was frozen.
It was a frozen throne.

308

Thirteen drummers thumping drums.
Thirteen drummers thumping drums.
Thirteen drummers thumping drums.

How many times can you say this in 10 seconds?

Thistle thorns stick.

It took Tom time to try to tote two totems to town.

Two ticket takers took a taxi.
Two ticket takers took a taxi.
Two ticket takers took a taxi.

Twelve tiny thread tweezers.
Twelve tiny thread tweezers.
Twelve tiny thread tweezers.

Twenty tender tree stumps.
Twenty tender tree stumps.
Twenty tender tree stumps.

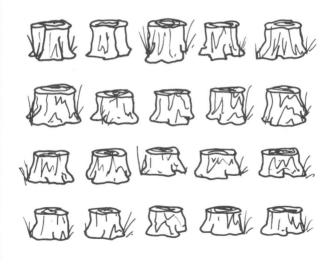

He says that a two twice-twisted twine
twisted twice twists twice as tight
as a one once-twisted twine twisted twice.
But I say that a two twice-twisted twine
twisted twice does not twist as tight
as a one once-twisted twine
twisted twice.

The tailor's tactics took twice the time.

Three thrushes rush thusly.

She shot three shy thrushes.

Thirty-three sly shy thrushes.
Thirty-three sly shy thrushes.
Thirty-three sly shy thrushes.

Theophilus Thistle, the successful
thistle-sifter,
Sifted sixty thistles through the thick
of his thumb.

Thick thistle sticks.
Thick thistle sticks.
Thick thistle sticks.

Six thick thistles stuck together.

Trent ties Ty's ties to trees to trick Ty.

TIME
CHALLENGE

How many times can you say this in 10 seconds?

Ted sent Stan ten tents.

A tree toad loved a she-toad
That lived up in a tree.
She was a three-toed tree toad,
But a two-toed toad was he.
The two-toed toad tried to win
The she-toad's friendly nod,
For the two-toed toad loved the ground
On which the three-toed tree toad trod.
But no matter how the two-toed
tree toad tried,
He could not please her whim.
In her three-toed bower,
With her three-toed power,
The three-toed she-toad vetoed him.

Ted threw Fred thirty-three free throws.

Three thick things
Three thick things.
Three thick things.

Three free through trains.
Three free through trains.
Three free through trains.

Truly rural.
Truly rural.
Truly rural.

Twixt six thick thumbs stick
six thick sticks.

Tim and Tom taped two tom-toms
together. Then Tim and Tom tapped the
tom-toms. Today, Tim's Mom tapped the
tom-toms too. But Tom's Mom thought
all that tom-tom taping was terrible.

320

Turtles waddle. Waiters toddle.

Tacky tractor trailer trucks.
Tacky tractor trailer trucks.
Tacky tractor trailer trucks.

Trill two true tunes to the troops.

Theo's throat throbs and thumps,
    thumps and throbs.

Thelma sings the theme song.

Twelve trim twin-track tapes.
Twelve trim twin-track tapes.
Twelve trim twin-track tapes.

An undertaker undertook
to undertake an undertaking.
The undertaking that
the undertaker undertook
was the hardest undertaking
the undertaker ever undertook
to undertake.

324

Underwood would wear underwear if
 Underwood knew where his underwear
 was.
Underwood's underwear was in
 Durwood's woods.
Underwood went into Durwood's woods
 and got his underwear.

Unique New York.
Unique New York.
Unique New York.

The U.S. twin-screw cruiser.
The U.S. twin-screw cruiser.
The U.S. twin-screw cruiser.

Unsung songs.
Unsung songs.
Unsung songs.

What veteran ventriloquist whistles?

Valuable valley villas.
Valuable valley villas.
Valuable valley villas.

The vicious visitors visited
the virtual village.

Vandals waxed Valerie's white van.

The wretched witch watched
  a walrus washing.
Did the wretched witch watch
  a walrus washing?
If the wretched witch watched
  a walrus washing,
Where's the washing walrus
  the wretched witch watched?

TIME CHALLENGE

*How many times can you
say this in 10 seconds?*

An itchy rich witch.

Which switch
is the witch's
switch?

These witch
twisters
have twisted
this witch.

If two witches watched two watches,
which witch would watch which watch?

Which wristwatch is a Swiss wristwatch?

Real wristwatch straps.
Real wristwatch straps.
Real wristwatch straps.

I wish I hadn't washed this wristwatch.
I washed all the wheels and the works.
Since this wristwatch got all washed,
Oh, how it jumps and jerks!

TIME CHALLENGE

*How many times can you
say this in 10 seconds?*

Wire rimmed wheels.

Hmmm......

Wyatt wondered
why the worn
wires weren't
wrapped right.

How much wood
would a woodchuck chuck
If a woodchuck could chuck wood?
He would chuck the wood
as much as he could
If a woodchuck could chuck wood.

Whether the weather be fine
Or whether the weather be not;
Whether the weather be cold
Or whether the weather be hot;
We'll weather the weather
Whatever the weather,
Whether we like it or not.

Wee Willie Winkie risks
three wishes.

White wings, round rings.
White wings, round rings.
White wings, round rings.

Wild wrens wing westward.

When Dwight White writes,
Dwight writes right.

Will won't write a real will.

Wally Wrinkle wriggles
his white, wrinkled wig.

One really wet red whale.

Wallie wrecked Randy's railway.

Weary railroad workers.

Which wishy-washy washerwoman
wants to watch?

Willie's awesome swallow follows
while Willie waddles.

If a warmly warbing warbler
warbles to another warmly
warbling warbler,
which warmly warbling warbler
warbles warmest?

Billy Wood said he would carry the wood
    through the woods,
And if Wood said he would,
    Wood would.

War-weary warriors.
War-weary warriors.
War-weary warriors.

Wilson whittles well-whittled wood whittle by whittle.

Xmas wrecks perplex and vex.

X-ray checks clear chests.

Ex-disk jockey.
Ex-disk jockey.
Ex-disk jockey.

The ex-egg examiner.
The ex-egg examiner.
The ex-egg examiner.

Agnes' "X"s are excellent.
Agnes excels in executing "X"s.

Yanking yellow yo-yos.
Yanking yellow yo-yos.
Yanking yellow yo-yos.

❋

Yellow leather, red feather.
Yellow leather, red feather.
Yellow leather, red feather.

Local yokel jokes.
Local yokel jokes.
Local yokel jokes.

Yesterday Yolanda yelled at Euwell.
Usually, Yuri yells at Euwell.

This is a zither.
Is this a zither?

This is Zoe's sister's zither.

Zithers slither slowly south.

Zizzi's zippy zipper zips.

Zack's backpack lacks Zach's snacks.

Index

351

If you liked this book, you'll love all the titles in this series:

- Little Giant Book of Insults & Putsdowns
- Little Giant Book of Jokes
- Little Giant Book of Kid's Games
- Little Giant Book of Knock-Knocks
- Little Giant Book of Optical Illisions
- Little Giant Book of Riddles
- Little Giant Book of Toungue Twisters
- Little Giant Book of "True" Ghost Stories
- Little Giant Book of Whodunits

Available at fine stores everywhere.